T0083166

Sarah Quartel Songbook

10 songs for mixed voices

MUSIC DEPARTMENT

OXFORD
UNIVERSITY PRESS

OXFORD
UNIVERSITY PRESS

Great Clarendon Street, Oxford OX2 6DP,
United Kingdom

Oxford University Press is a department of the University of Oxford.
It furthers the University's objective of excellence in research, scholarship,
and education by publishing worldwide. Oxford is a registered trade mark of
Oxford University Press in the UK and in certain other countries

This collection © Oxford University Press 2021

Sarah Quartel has asserted her right under the Copyright, Designs
and Patents Act, 1988, to be identified as the Composer of these Works

Database right Oxford University Press (maker)

First published 2021

All rights reserved. No part of this publication may be reproduced,
stored in a retrieval system, or transmitted, in any form or by any means,
without the prior permission in writing of Oxford University Press

Permission to perform this work in public (except in the course of divine worship)
should normally be obtained from a local performing right licensing organization,
unless the owner or the occupier of the premises being used already holds
a licence from such an organization. Likewise, permission to make and
exploit a recording of these works should be obtained from a
local mechanical copyright licensing organization

Enquiries concerning reproduction outside the scope of the above
should be directed to the Music Rights Department, Oxford University Press,
at music.permissions.uk@oup.com or at the address above

ISBN 978–0–19–355104–6

Music and text origination by Katie Johnston
Printed in Great Britain on acid-free paper by
Halstan & Co. Ltd, Amersham, Bucks.

Contents

Introduction	iv
Wide Open Spaces	1
Sing, my Child	10
All the way home	17
How can I keep from singing?	24
'Hope' is the thing with feathers	35
Swept Away	42
Voice on the Wind	57
I know a bank where the wild thyme blows	68
One of these Days	74
The Parting Glass	88

Introduction

It is such a pleasure to see these pieces together in one collection. We begin with 'Wide Open Spaces', which received its premiere under the baton of Bob Chilcott at the American Choral Directors Association National Conference in 2014. A year later, Bob included 'I know a bank where the wild thyme blows' in his edited collection of Shakespeare settings, *Shall I compare thee?*. I would not be where I am today without his tremendous support, mentorship, and advocacy!

A choir of nearly 500 singers premiered 'Sing, my Child' at the 2016 International Choral Kathaumixw in British Columbia and, in 2018, the SATB version of 'Voice on the Wind' was premiered by Gemischter Chor ANGUSTA of Japan. "Hope' is the thing with feathers' was written for Ely Consort in England, and this mixed-voice version of 'All the way home' was commissioned by Penn High School in Indiana.

This arrangement of 'How can I keep from singing?' was completed when I was pregnant with my son in 2017 and was the first piece I sang to him after he was born. 'Swept Away' also holds a special place in my heart, as it was written for my husband while he was deployed with the Royal Canadian Navy. 'The Parting Glass' is dedicated to a friend as a welcome home from his own deployment with the Canadian Armed Forces.

Although published here for the first time, 'One of these Days' may be the oldest song in this collection. It was originally written for a sensational Finnish pop singer and has found new life in this six-part *a cappella* arrangement.

As I look at the titles included in this collection and remember the people who have inspired them, I am reminded that choral music-making holds a tremendous power to connect and unite us. I am thankful to every person who inspired these pieces and grateful to Robyn Elton and Laura Jones for bringing this collection to life.

Sarah Quartel
March 2021

Commissioned by the American Choral Directors Association
for the Middle School/Junior High School Boys' Honor Choir, Bob Chilcott conductor,
Salt Lake City, Utah, February 28, 2014.
Sponsored by Classical Movements, Inc.

Wide Open Spaces

Words and music by
SARAH QUARTEL
(b. 1982)

Duration: 3 mins

Also available in versions for TTBB and piano (ISBN 978–0–19–341339–9) and SSAA and piano (ISBN 978–0–19–355096–4).

© Oxford University Press 2014. Photocopying this copyright material is ILLEGAL.

18
There's part of my jour - ney that's yet to be
24
mf
found. With life all a - round us
mf
30
and so much to see, Ad - ven-ture is
36
call - ing, It's call-ing to me.

42
Out in the wide o - pen spa - ces a - round me.
mp
48
S./A.
T./B.
TENORS & BASSES unis. mf
With big sky a - bove
mf
54
T./B.
me, I'm on my way,
sim.
60
Scan-ning the ho - ri - zon of a brand new day.

66
mf
S.
A.
Feet to the earth now,
T.
B.
mf
72
there's no turn-ing back.
In-to the world
78
now,
look at me, look at me go!

84
f
Out in the wide o - pen spa-ces a - round me,
f
f
f
90
out in the wide o - pen spa-ces a -
96
mf
-round me.
But as I
mf
mf

102
jour - ney out I look with - in and
sim.
108
see The spa-ces in - side of me yet to
114
be filled, Filled with what I have seen
f
f
f
8vb

120
mf
and what I will be. Oh! doo doo n doo
8vb
126
doo n doo doo doo doo n doo doo doo doo doo n doo doo n doo doo
mf
mf
131
f
doo I'm fill - ing the wide o - pen spa - ces in -
f
f

136
-side of me With some-thing I love,
142
some - thing I would like to be, be, be!
148
Fill-ing the wide o - pen spa-ces in - side of me,

154
unis. mp
Fill - ing the wide
unis.
mp
mp
160
rit.
o - pen spa - ces with - in me.
rit.
166
rit.
rit.

Commissioned for the 2016 International Choral Kathaumixw
Paul Cummings, Artistic Director

Sing, my Child

Words and music by
SARAH QUARTEL

Light and dancing ♪ = 144

DRUM*

SOPRANO SOLO
mf

SOPRANO
ALTO

Sing for the pro-mise in each new morn-ing. Sing for the hope in a

TENOR SOLO
mf

TENOR
BASS

Sing for the hope in a

4

new day dawn-ing. All a - round is beau - ty bright!

new day dawn-ing. All a - round is beau - ty bright!

7

D.

Wake in the morn-ing and sing, my child, sing, my child.

Wake in the morn-ing and sing, my child, sing, my child.

Duration: 4.5 mins

* A cajón or large djembe is preferred, but any hand drum with a deep, rich sound will work well.

Also available in a version for SSAA and hand drum (ISBN 978–0–19–353024–9).

© Oxford University Press 2017. Photocopying this copyright material is ILLEGAL.

10
f
TUTTI
f
S.
A.
Sing for the pro-mise in each new morn-ing. Sing for the hope in a
TUTTI
T.
B.
f
13
new day dawn-ing. All a - round is beau-ty bright!
16
Wake in the morn-ing and sing, my child, sing, my child,
19
sub. p
mf
sub. p
mf
sing, my child, sing, my child,
sub. p
mf
sing, my child, oh sing, my child, oh sing, my child, oh sing, my child, oh

23
p
p
sing, my child. ah
p
sing, my child, oh sing, my child, oh sing, my child, oh sing, my child.
27
f
f
Dance in the joy of the day un - fold-ing. Dance as you work and
f
30
dance as you're learn-ing. All a - round is beau-ty bright!
33
Take in the day and dance, my child, dance, my child,

36
poco rit.
p
dance, my child, dance, my child.
p
Strong, like a hymn ♩ = 96
39
mf
But when trou - bles come and wor - ry is
mf
44
all that can be found, gath - er your strength and
49
mp
rit.
hear your voice. Sing, my child.
mp

Tempo I ♪ = 144
54
D.
f
Laugh in the cool and the fresh of the ev'n - ing. Laugh in your tri - umph,
Laugh, laugh, oh laugh, my child, laugh, laugh, oh laugh, my child, laugh, laugh, oh laugh, my child,
57
laugh in suc-ceed-ing. All a - round is beau-ty bright!
laugh, laugh, oh laugh, my child, laugh, laugh, oh laugh, my child, laugh, laugh, oh laugh, my child,
60
Peace in the still-ness and
mf
mp
Rest in the ev'n - ing and laugh, my child. Peace,
laugh, laugh, oh laugh, my child, laugh, laugh, my child.
63
dark of the night. Peace in the dreams of your si - lent de - lights.
peace, peace, peace,

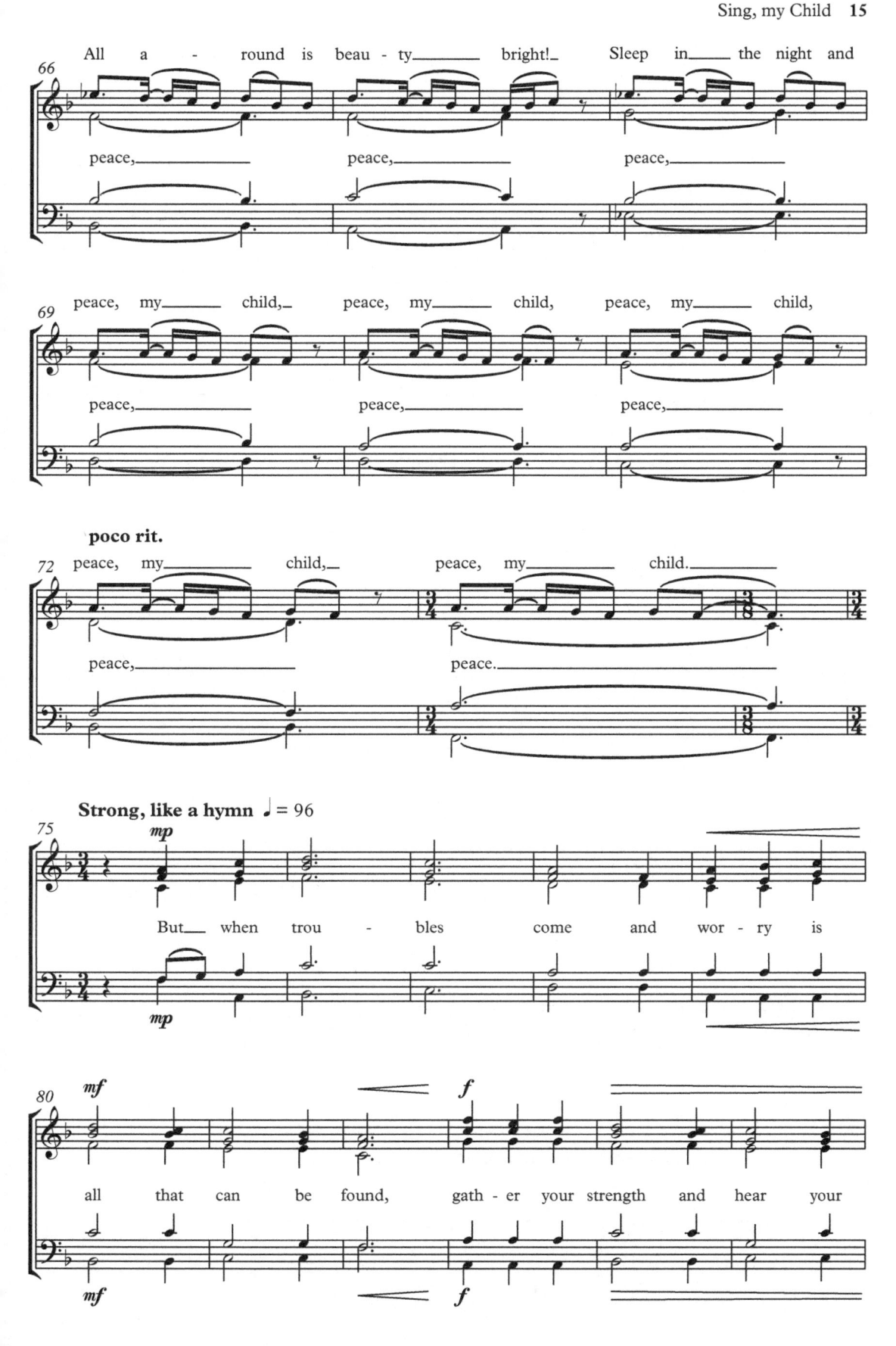
66
All a - round is beau - ty bright! Sleep in the night and
peace, peace, peace,
69
peace, my child, peace, my child, peace, my child,
peace, peace, peace,
poco rit.
72
peace, my child, peace, my child.
peace, peace.
Strong, like a hymn ♩ = 96
75
mp
But when trou - bles come and wor - ry is
mp
80
mf
f
all that can be found, gath - er your strength and hear your
mf
f

86
mp
mf
voice. Sing, my child. Dance, my
mp
mf
92
f
child. Laugh, my child.
f
98
p sub.
Peace, my child.
p sub.
♩ = ♪
rit.
SOPRANO AND TENOR SOLO
104
mp
(8)
Peace, my child, oh, peace, my child.
p
oo
oo
p

In memory of Kassidy
Commissioned by Viva Voce of Penn High School Choir, Mishawaka, IN
Andrew Nemeth, Director

All the way home

Text written and inspired by
members of the Radcliffe Ladies' Choir as they
reflected on their motto, "friendship through singing"

SARAH QUARTEL

Duration: 3.5 mins

Also available in versions for SSA and piano (ISBN 978–0–19–352590–0) and solo voice and piano (high voice ISBN 978–0–19–354742–1)/ low voice ISBN 978–0–19–354743–8).

© Oxford University Press 2018 and 2021. Photocopying this copyright material is ILLEGAL.

23
mf
joy - ful, with har - mon - ies sing me all the way
- long,
mf
mf
30
home with a song in my heart. All the way home
36
bright - en my path and car - ry me on,

42
mp
poco rit.
all the way home.
mp
poco rit.
mp
49
mf
a tempo
There's a beau - ti - ful pow'r in what we bring, there's
mf
a tempo
mf
55
mf
strength in the glor - ious song we sing. Eas - ing all
mf
mf

61
trou - bles, calm-ing all fears, joy - ful, with har - mon-ies sing
68
me all the way home with a song in my heart. All the way
75
home bright-en my path and car - ry me on,

82
mp
all the way home.
mp
mp
poco meno mosso
89
mf
ah
mf
poco meno mosso
mf
95 unis. p
/B.
Eve - ning brings a shin - ing star, her an - cient an - thems
p

102
p
from a - far.
Si - lence be - low, her song in the sky.
p
rit.
a tempo
110
unis.
f
S./A.
Joy - ful with har-mon-ies sing me all the way home with a
T./B.
f
rit.
a tempo
f
116
song in my heart. All the way home

122
mf
bright-en my path and car - ry me on, all the way
mf
mf
poco rit.
rit.
129
home, all the way
poco rit.
rit.
a tempo
molto rit.
136
mp
home.
mp
a tempo
molto rit.
mp

How can I keep from singing?

Text unattributed (adapted)

ROBERT LOWRY (1826–99)
arr. SARAH QUARTEL

Duration: 4 mins

Also available in a version for SSAA unaccompanied (ISBN 978–0–19–352208–4).

© Oxford University Press 2017 and 2018. Photocopying this copyright material is ILLEGAL.

18
TUTTI
mf
My life flows on in
how can I keep from sing-ing, how can I keep from sing-ing! How can I keep from sing-ing,
how can I keep from sing-ing, how can I keep from sing-ing! How can I keep from sing-ing,
how can I keep from sing-ing, how can I keep from sing-ing! How can I keep from sing-ing,
21
end-less song a-bove earth's la - - men-ta-tions, I
how can I keep from sing-ing! How can I keep from sing-ing, how can I keep from sing-ing!
how can I keep from sing-ing! How can I keep from sing-ing, how can I keep from sing-ing!
how can I keep from sing-ing! How can I keep from sing-ing, how can I keep from sing-ing!

24
hear the real though far-off tune that hails a new cre-
How can I keep from sing-ing, how can I keep from sing - ing! How can I keep from sing-ing,
How can I keep from sing-ing, how can I keep from sing - ing! How can I keep from sing-ing,
How can I keep from sing-ing, how can I keep from sing - ing! How can I keep from sing-ing,
27
f
-a - tion. Through all the tu - - mult and the strife I
how can I keep from sing - ing! How can I keep from sing-ing, how can I keep from sing - ing!
how can I keep from sing - ing! How can I keep from sing-ing, how can I keep from sing - ing!
how can I keep from sing - ing! How can I keep from sing-ing, how can I keep from sing - ing!

30
hear its mu - - sic ring-ing. It sounds an e - - cho
How can I keep from sing-ing, how can I keep from sing-ing! How can I keep from sing-ing,
How can I keep from sing-ing, how can I keep from sing-ing! How can I keep from sing-ing,
How can I keep from sing-ing, how can I keep from sing-ing! How can I keep from sing-ing,
33
mf
in my soul, how can I keep from sing-ing?
how can I keep from sing - ing! How can I keep from, how can I keep from sing-ing,
how can I keep from sing - ing! How can I keep from, how can I keep from sing-ing,
how can I keep from sing - ing! How can I keep from, how can I keep from sing-ing,

36
f
How can I keep from sing - ing! While
how can I keep from sing - ing, how can I keep from sing - ing!
how can I keep from sing - ing, how can I keep from sing - ing!
how can I keep from sing - ing, how can I keep from sing - ing!
39
though the tem - pest loud-ly roars, I hear the truth, it
Though tem - pests roar loud - ly, I hear the
Though tem - pests roar loud - ly, I hear the
Though tem - pests roar loud - ly, I hear the

* *close*, the verb, with a 'z' sound

48
in - most calm while to that rock I'm cling - ing. Since love is Lord of
in - most calm while to that rock I'm cling - ing. Since love is Lord of
in - most calm while to that rock I'm cling - ing. Since love is Lord of
in - most calm while to that rock I'm cling - ing. Since love is Lord of

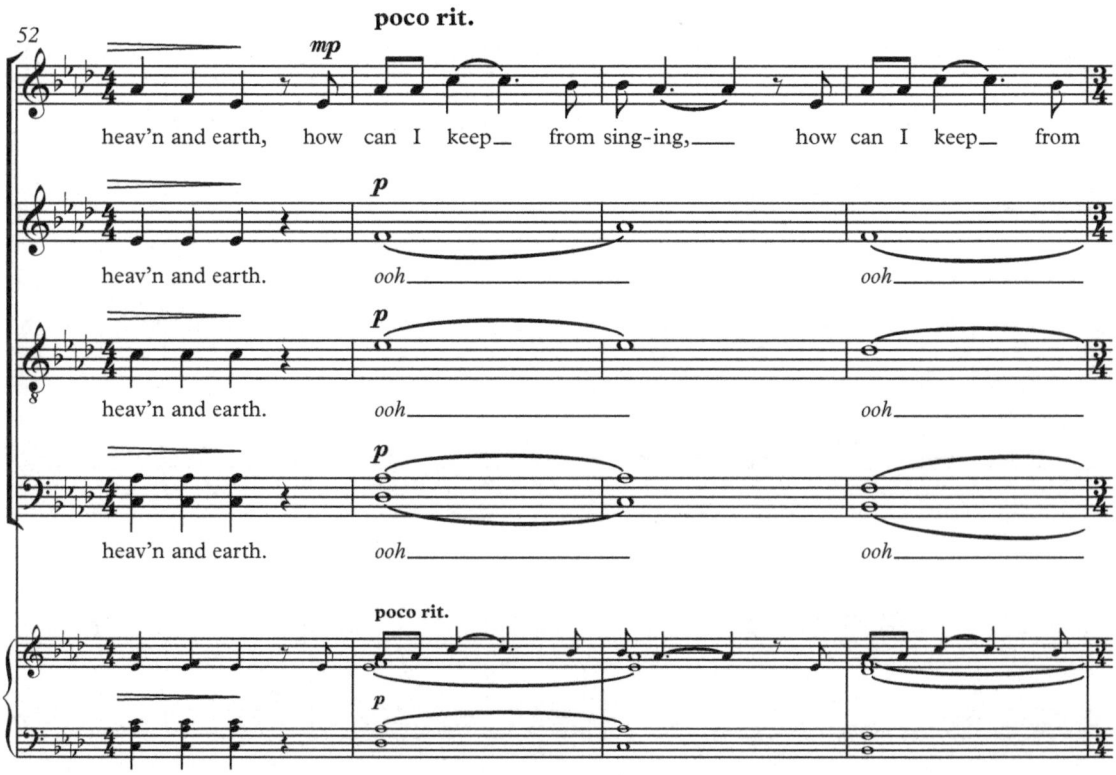
52
poco rit.
mp
heav'n and earth, how can I keep from sing-ing, how can I keep from
p
heav'n and earth. ooh ooh
p
heav'n and earth. ooh ooh
p
heav'n and earth. ooh ooh
poco rit.
p

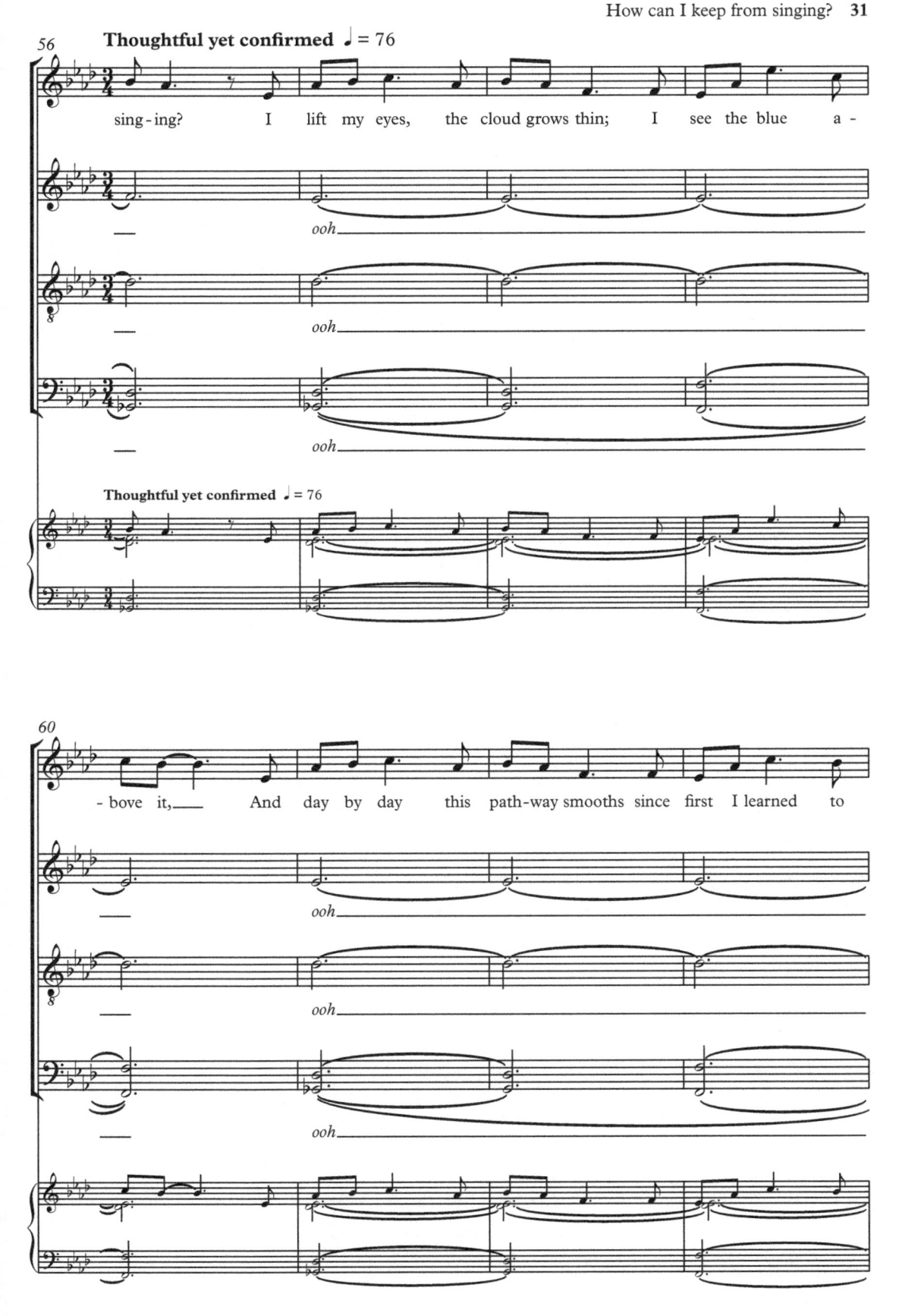
56
Thoughtful yet confirmed ♩ = 76
sing - ing? I lift my eyes, the cloud grows thin; I see the blue a -
ooh
ooh
ooh
Thoughtful yet confirmed ♩ = 76
60
- bove it, And day by day this path-way smooths since first I learned to
ooh
ooh
ooh

a little more movement, with growing excitement
64
cresc.
love it. The peace of love makes fresh my heart, a
mp cresc.
Peace of love makes fresh my heart, a
mp cresc.
Peace of love makes fresh my heart, a
mp cresc.
Peace of love makes fresh my heart, a
a little more movement, with growing excitement
mp cresc.
molto rit.
67
f
foun-tain ev - - er spring - ing; All things are mine in
f
foun - tain ev - er spring - ing; All things are mine in
f
foun - tain ev - er spring - ing; All things are mine in
f
foun - tain ev - er spring - ing; All things are mine in
molto rit.
f

Sure and confirmed ♩ = 96
How can I keep from
70
div.
love and joy! How can I keep from
love and joy! How can I keep from sing - ing,
love and joy! How can I keep from sing - ing,
love and joy! How can I keep from sing - ing,
Sure and confirmed ♩ = 96
sing - ing, how can I keep from
72
sing - ing, how can I keep from
how can I keep from sing - ing, how can I keep from sing - ing,
how can I keep from sing - ing, how can I keep from sing - ing,
how can I keep from sing - ing, how can I keep from sing - ing,

* small notes solo (optional)

for Ely Consort

'Hope' is the thing with feathers

Emily Dickinson (1830–86)

SARAH QUARTEL

Duration: 3.5 mins

© Oxford University Press 2019. Photocopying this copyright material is ILLEGAL.

7
per - ches in the soul And sings the tune with-
per - ches in the soul And sings the tune with -
per - ches in the soul And sings the tune with -
poco rit.
a tempo
10
mp
- out the words And ne - ver stops at all.
p
- out the words And ne - ver stops at all.
p
- out the words And ne - ver stops at all.
poco rit.
a tempo
mp

13
T.
B.
mf
And
mf
16
S.
A.
(stagger breathing)
p
ah
T.
B.
sweet-est in the gale is heard And sore must be the
19
mf
storm That could a - bash the lit - tle bird That
mf

22
p
mp
I've
kept so ma - ny warm.
25
heard it in the chill - est land And on the strang - est
28
mf
div. f
S.
sea; ne - ver, ne - ver,
A.
sea; Yet, ne - ver, ne - ver, ne - ver,
T.
B.
sea; Yet, ne - ver, ne - ver,

31
ff
unis.
ne - ver, in ex - trem - i - ty, It
ff
ne - ver, ne - ver, in ex - trem - i - ty, It
ff
ne - ver, in ex - trem - i - ty, It
ff
poco rit.
a tempo
34
mf
asked a crumb of me.
mf
asked a crumb of me.
mf
asked a crumb of me.
poco rit.
a tempo
mp

38
S.
mp
'Hope' is the thing with fea - thers,
A.
T.
B.
41
mf
hope, hope,
mp
'Hope' is the thing with fea - thers,
mf
'hope' is the thing with
mp
mf
'Hope' is the thing with fea - thers, with
mp
mf
'Hope' is the thing,

44
mp
with fea - thers, with fea - thers, with
fea - thers, with fea - thers, with fea - thers, with
fea - thers, with fea - thers, with fea - thers, with
'hope' is the thing with fea - thers, with fea - thers, with
47
rit.
p
fea - thers, with fea - thers, with fea - thers.
fea - thers, with fea - thers, with fea - thers.
fea - thers, with fea - thers, with fea - thers.
fea - thers, with fea - thers, with fea - thers.
rit.
p

for the sailor I love

Swept Away

Words and music by
SARAH QUARTEL

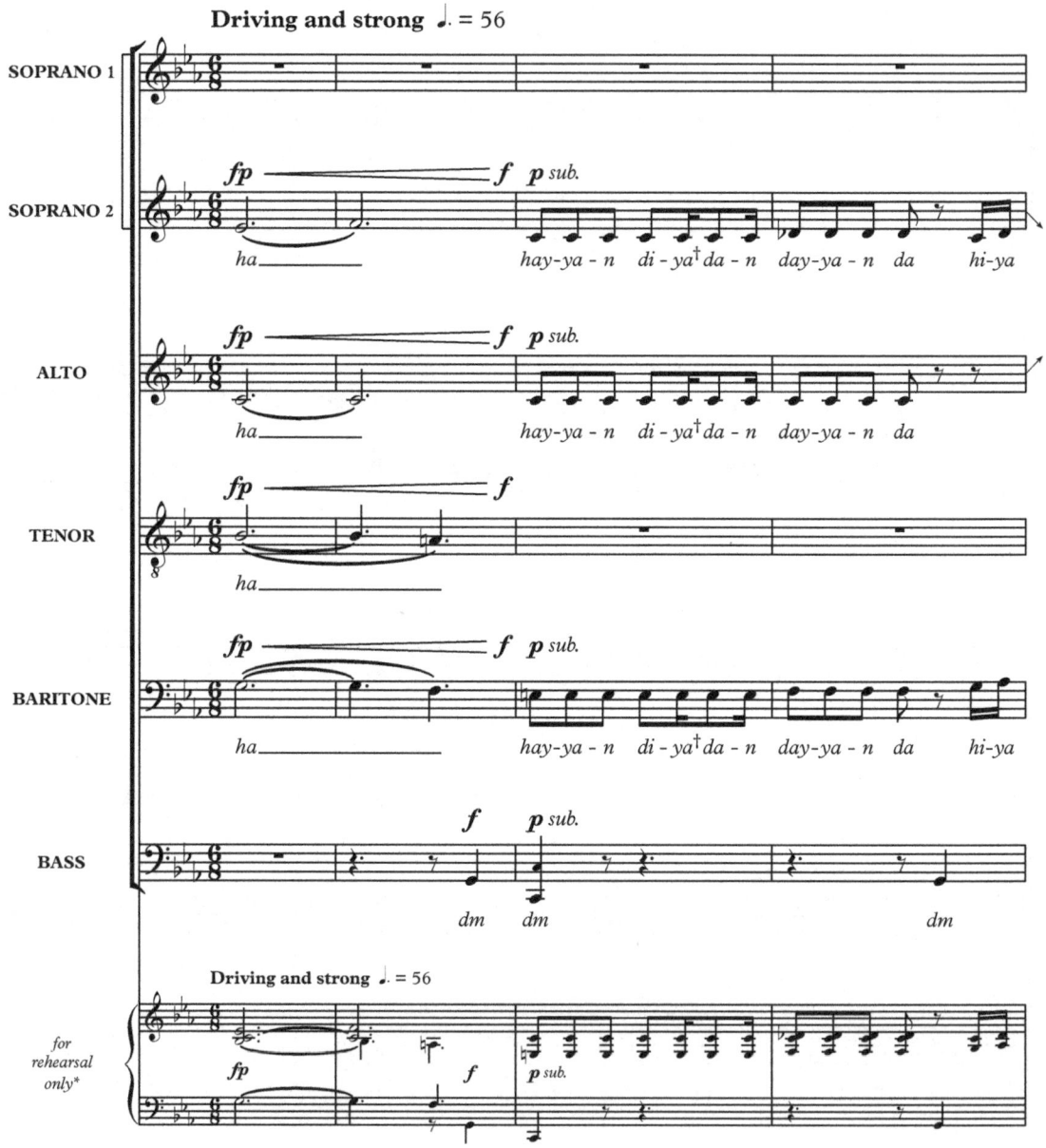

Duration: 4 mins

† pronounced 'dye-ya'

* The piano reduction includes the rhythmic accompanying parts throughout; for reasons of playability, melodic lines are sometimes omitted.

© Oxford University Press 2019. Photocopying this copyright material is ILLEGAL.

5
mp
hay-ya - n di - ya da - n day-ya - n da hay-ya - n di - ya da - n day-ya - n da hi-ya
hay-ya - n di - ya da - n day-ya - n da hay-ya - n di - ya da - n day-ya - n da hi-ya
dm dm dm dm dm dm dm
9
mf
hay - ya - n di - ya da - n day - ya - n da hay - ya - n di - ya da - n
hi - ya
hay - ya - n di - ya da - n day - ya - n da hay - ya - n di - ya da - n
dm dm dm dm doo doo doo doo doo doo doo

* The vowel sound for 'hae' and 'yae' should be 'a' as in 'cat', with North American pronunciation.

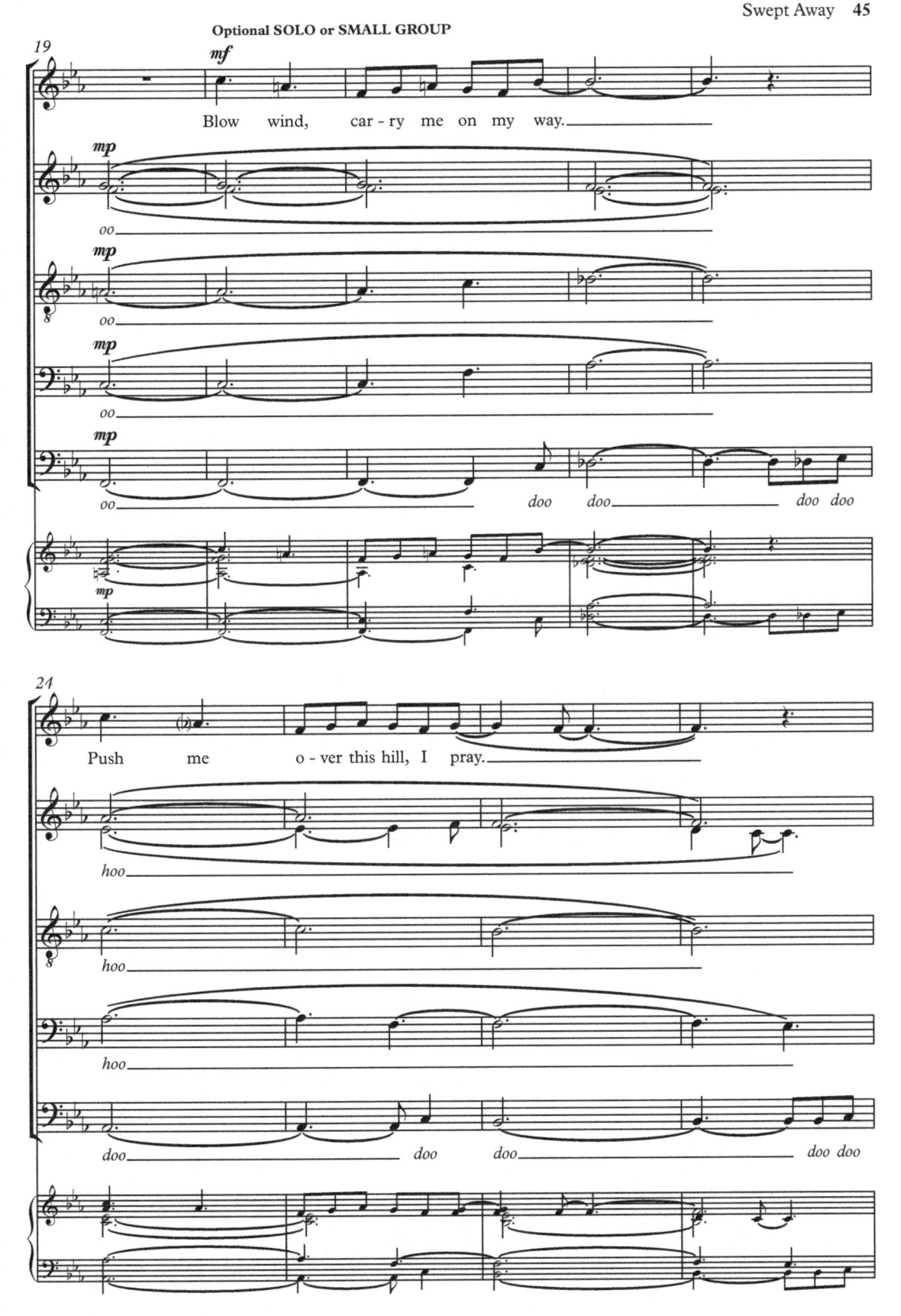
Optional SOLO or SMALL GROUP
19
mf
Blow wind, car - ry me on my way.
mp
oo
mp
oo
mp
oo
mp
oo doo doo doo doo
mp
24
Push me o - ver this hill, I pray.
hoo
hoo
hoo
doo doo doo doo doo

28
Al - ways mov - ing and al - ways strong,
hoo
hoo
hoo
hoo
doo doo doo doo doo
32
take me where I must be - long.
f
hoo ya hay - ya - n di - ya da - n day - ya - n da
p
f
hoo ya hay - ya - n di - ya da - n day - ya - n da
p
f
hoo doo doo
p
f
doo doo doo doo doo
f

36
(TUTTI) mf
hae ee yae
mp
doo doo doo doo doo doo doo doo doo doo doo doo-n doo doo doo doo doo doo doo
mp
hi - ya ya - n da hi -
mp
doo doo doo doo doo doo doo doo doo doo doo doo-n doo doo doo doo doo doo doo
mp
doo doo doo doo doo doo
mp
39
ee yae hae ee yae
doo doo doo doo doo doo doo doo doo doo doo doo doo doo doo doo-n
-ya hn da hi - ya ya - n
doo doo doo doo doo doo doo doo doo doo doo doo doo doo doo doo-n
doo doo doo doo doo doo doo doo

42
f
hae yae
mf
doo doo doo doo doo doo doo doo doo doo doo
hay - ya - n di - ya da - n
da hi - - ya hn da hi - ya
doo doo doo doo doo doo doo doo doo doo doo
hay - ya - n di - ya da - n
doo doo doo doo doo doo doo doo doo
45
ee hae
day - ya - n da hi-ya hay - ya - n di - ya da - n day - ya - n da
ya - n da hi - - ya hn da
day - ya - n da hi-ya hay - ya - n di - ya da - n day - ya - n da
doo doo doo doo doo doo doo doo doo doo doo doo doo

48
yae ee yae hae
port.
hay-ya-n di-ya da-n day-ya-n da hi-ya hay-ya-n di-ya da-n day-ya-n da
hi-ya ya-n da hi-ya hn da
hay-ya-n di-ya da-n day-ya-n da hi-ya hay-ya-n di-ya da-n day-ya-n da
doo doo doo doo doo doo doo doo doo doo doo doo doo doo doo doo doo
Optional SOLO or SMALL GROUP
52
mf
Ground-ed af-ter the storm-y wind.
mp
oo
mp
oo
mp
oo
mp
oo doo doo doo doo
mp

57
Plant - ed here at my jour-ney's end.
hoo
hoo
hoo
doo doo doo doo doo
61
Twist - ed roots now deep and strong
hi - ya - n
hoo
hoo
hoo
doo doo doo ha

(TUTTI)
65
f
hold me here where I must be - long. But in
ah ya hay-ya - n di - ya da - n day - ya - n da
ah ya hay-ya - n di - ya da - n day - ya - n da
ah oo doo
ya oo doo doo
69
you I am swept a-way, breath-less and swept a-way, leav - ing me hap - py and
You, I am breath - less, hap - - py and
You, I am breath - less, hap - - py and
You, I am breath - less, hap - - py and
doo doo doo doo doo doo doo doo doo doo doo doo

72
help - less. Here I am swept a-way, caught in a cur-rent so strong.
help - less. Here, in a cur - rent so
help - less. Here, in a cur - rent so
help - less. Here, in a cur - rent, oh,
doo doo doo doo doo doo doo doo doo doo doo doo
75
S.1
Here I am swept a-way,
S.2
strong, caught in a cur-rent so strong. Oh, here, I am
A.
strong, caught in a cur-rent so strong. Here I am swept a-way,
T.
strong, caught in a cur-rent so strong. Oh, here, I am
BAR.
caught in a cur - rent so strong. Oh, here, I am
B.
Caught in a cur - rent so strong. doo doo doo doo doo doo doo

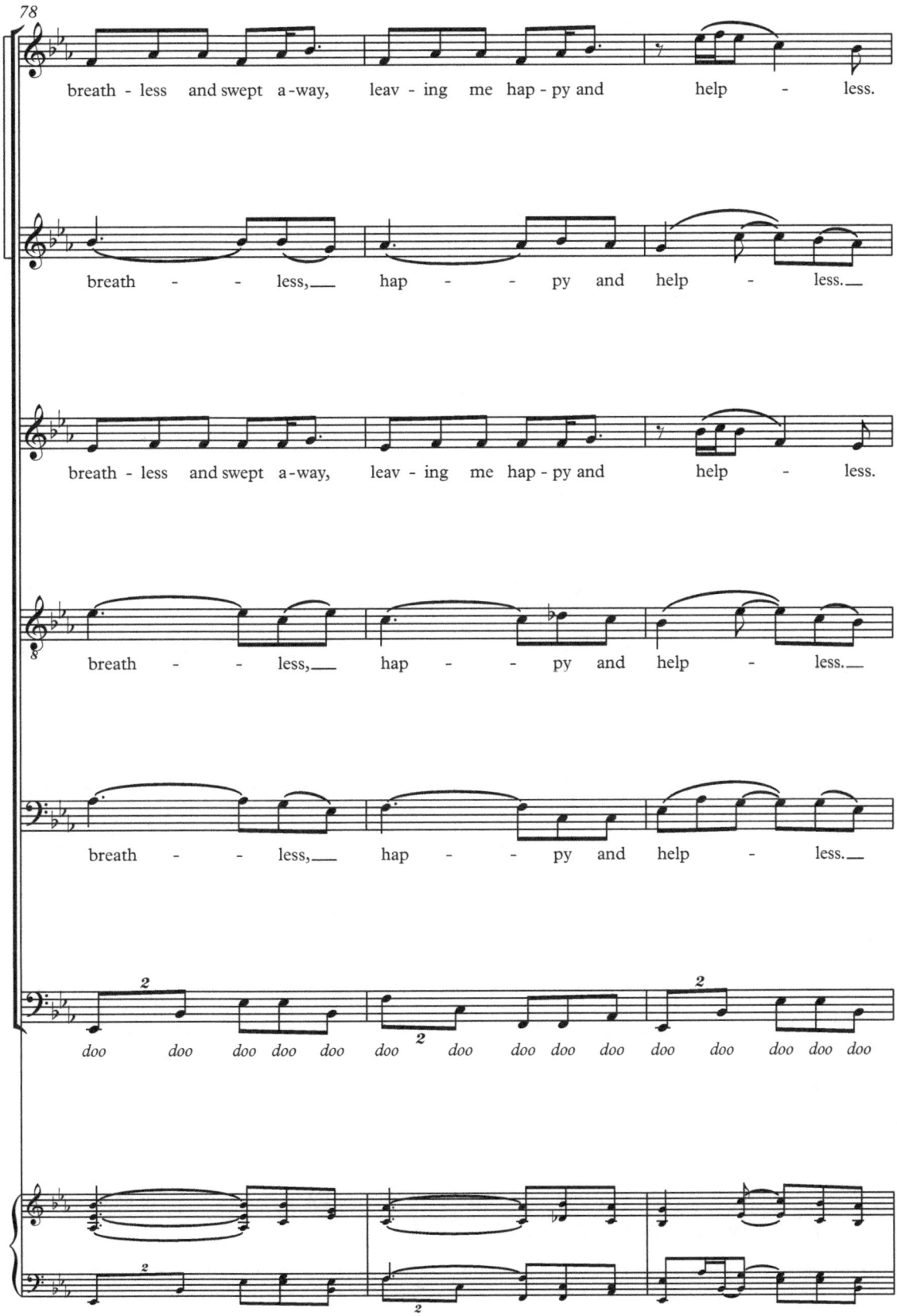
78
breath - less and swept a-way, leav - ing me hap - py and help - less.
breath - - less, hap - - py and help - less.
breath - less and swept a-way, leav - ing me hap - py and help - less.
breath - - less, hap - - py and help - less.
breath - - less, hap - - py and help - less.
doo doo doo doo doo doo doo doo doo doo doo doo doo doo doo

81
Here I am swept a-way, caught in a cur-rent so strong.
Here, in a cur-rent so strong.
Here I am swept a-way, caught in a cur-rent so strong.
Here, in a cur-rent so strong.
Here, in a cur-rent so strong.
doo doo doo doo doo doo doo doo doo doo doo
84
S.2
A.
mp
doo doo doo doo doo doo doo doo doo doo doo doo-n doo doo doo doo doo doo doo
T.
mf
hi - ya ya - n da hi -
BAR.
mp
doo doo doo doo doo doo doo doo doo doo doo doo-n doo doo doo doo doo doo doo
B.
mp
doo doo doo doo doo doo doo doo
mp

87
doo doo doo doo doo doo doo doo doo doo doo doo doo doo doo doo-n
-ya hn da hi - ya ya - n
doo doo doo doo doo doo doo doo doo doo doo doo doo doo doo doo-n
doo doo doo doo doo doo doo
90
f
hae - ee yae
mf
doo doo doo doo doo doo doo doo doo doo doo doo hay - ya - n di - ya da - n
da hi - - ya hn da hi - ya
mf
doo doo doo doo doo doo doo doo doo doo doo doo hay - ya - n di - ya da - n
mf
doo doo doo doo doo doo doo doo doo
mf

93
hae-ee yae hae-ee yae hae-ee yae hae-ee yae
day-ya-n da hi-ya hay-ya-n di-ya da-n day-ya-n da hay-ya-n di-ya da-n
ya-n da hi-ya hn da hi-ya
day-ya-n da hi-ya hay-ya-n di-ya da-n day-ya-n da hay-ya-n di-ya da-n
doo doo doo doo doo doo doo doo doo doo doo doo doo doo doo
97
ff
hae-ee yae hae yae
f
day-ya-n da hi-ya hay-ya-n di-ya da-n ha ha ha hoo
f
ya-n da hi-ya hn da hoo
f
day-ya-n da hi-ya hay-ya-n di-ya da-n ha ha ha hoo
f
doo doo doo doo doo doo doo doo doo doo doo hoo
f

Commissioned by Gemischter Chor ANGUSTA, Sapporo City, Japan, and their artistic director Takayuki Fukuda

Voice on the Wind

Words and music by
SARAH QUARTEL

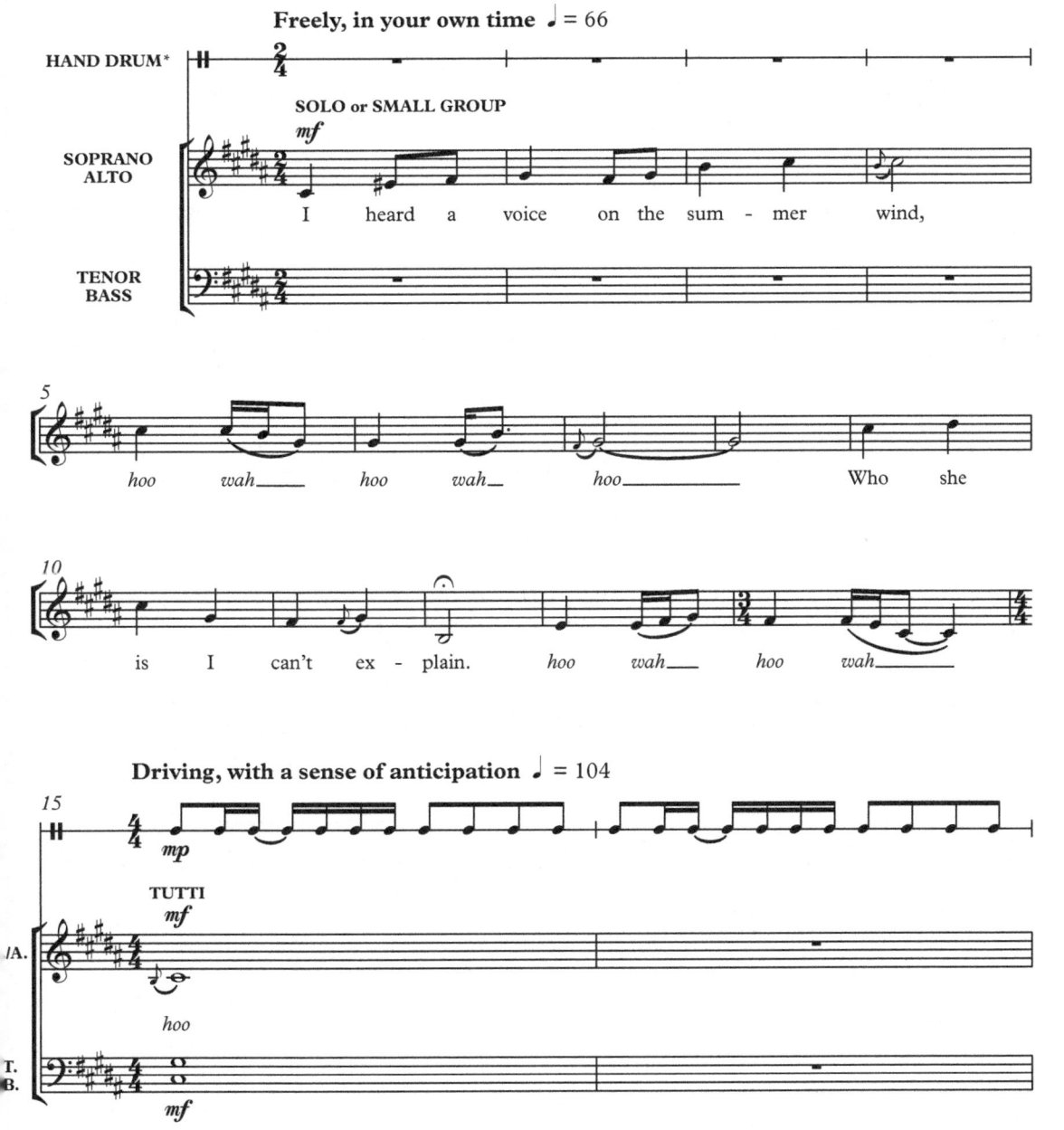

Duration: 4 mins

* Alternatively a bodhrán may be used.

Also available in a version for SSAA and hand drum (ISBN 978–0–19–341013–8).

© Oxford University Press 2015 and 2018. Photocopying this copyright material is ILLEGAL.

17
BASSES
mp
I heard a voice on the sum-mer wind,
hoo wah hoo wah hoo
20
mp
T.
B.
Blow-ing free and blow-ing wild.
23
mf
mf
I heard a voice on the sum-mer wind,
hoo wah hoo wah hoo wah hoo
mf
26
hoo wah hoo wah hoo

29
S.
Strength and spi - rit in her song.
A.
Strength and spi - rit in her song.
T.
B.
Strength and spi - rit in her song.
31
hoo wah hoo wah hoo wah hoo
hoo wah hoo wah hoo wah hoo
hoo wah hoo wah hoo wah hoo
33
hoo wah hoo wah hoo wah hoo
hoo wah hoo wah hoo
hoo wah ya hoo wah ya
hoo wah ya hoo wah ya

35
f
hoo wah_ hoo wah hoo wah hoo
hoo wah_ hoo wah hoo
hoo wah___ ya
hoo wah___ ya
hoo wah___ ya
hoo wah___ ya
37
Strength and spi - rit in her song.___
hoo wah___ ya
hoo wah___ ya
hoo wah___ ya
hoo wah___ ya
39
mp
hoo wah hoo wah hoo wah hoo
dun dun dun
hoo wah___ ya
hoo wah___ ya
dun dun___ dun
hoo wah___ ya
hoo wah___ ya
dun dun___ dun

42
mf
dun dun I heard a voice on the sum - mer wind,
mf
dun dun dun I heard a voice on the sum - mer wind,
mf
dun dun dun I heard a voice on the sum - mer wind,
44
mf
hoo wah hoo wah hoo
hoo wah hoo wah hoo
hoo wah hoo wah hoo
47
With a song I seem to know. hoo wah hoo wah hoo wah hoo
With a song I seem to know. hoo wah hoo wah hoo wah hoo
With a song I seem to know. hoo wah hoo wah hoo wah hoo

50
I heard a voice on the sum - mer wind,
I heard a voice on the sum - mer wind,
I heard a voice on the sum - mer wind,
52
hoo wah_ hoo wah hoo wah
hoo wah_ hoo wah hoo wah
hoo wah_ hoo wah hoo wah
55
Sounds fa - mil - iar like my own.
Sounds fa - mil - iar like my own.
TENORS
Sounds fa - mil - iar like my own.

57
mf
f
S.
mp
hoo wah hoo wah hoo wah hoo hoo
A.
p
hoo wah hoo wah hoo wah hoo hoo wah hoo wah hoo
T.
mp
hoo wah hoo wah hoo
B.
p
hoo wah hoo wah hoo wah hoo hoo wah hoo wah hoo wah hoo
59
A.
f
hoo wah ya hoo wah
T.
f
hoo wah hoo wah hoo wah hoo hoo wah hoo wah hoo
B.
f
hoo wah ya hoo wah ya
61
hoo wah ya hoo wah
hoo wah hoo wah hoo wah hoo hoo wah hoo wah hoo
hoo wah ya hoo wah ya

63
S.
Sounds fa - mil - iar like my own
p
A.
hoo wah ya hoo wah ya
p
T.
B.
hoo wah ya hoo wah ya
65
p
mp
mp
div.
hoo wah oh wah oo
mp
mf
hoo wah I heard a voice on the
p
mp
dun dun dun dun dun dun oo
68
wah oh
sum - mer wind, on the sum - mer wind, on the sum - mer wind,
wah oh

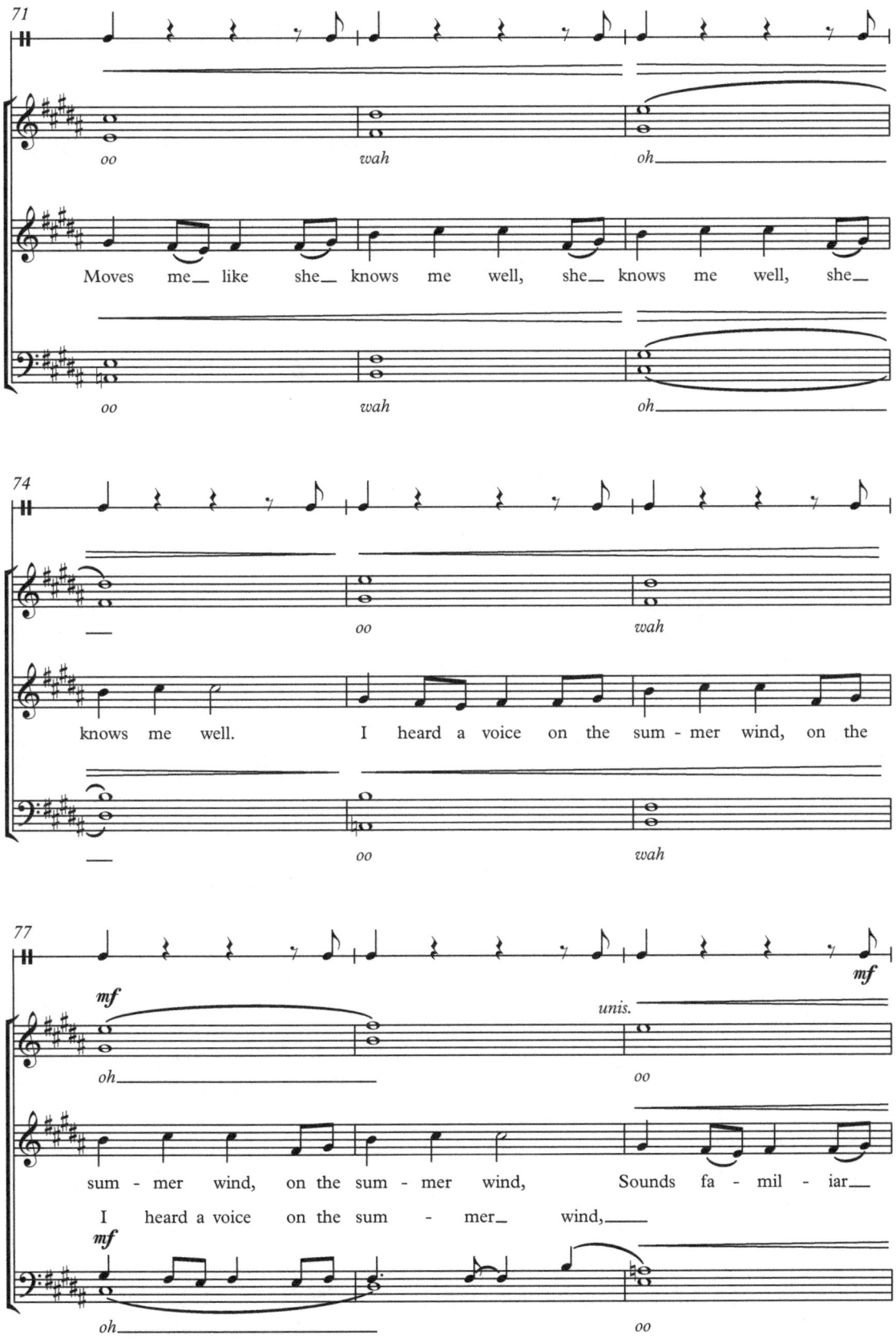
71
oo wah oh
Moves me like she knows me well, she knows me well, she
oo wah oh
74
oo wah
knows me well. I heard a voice on the sum - mer wind, on the
oo wah
77
mf
mf
unis.
oh oo
sum - mer wind, on the sum - mer wind, Sounds fa - mil - iar
I heard a voice on the sum - mer wind,
mf
oh oo

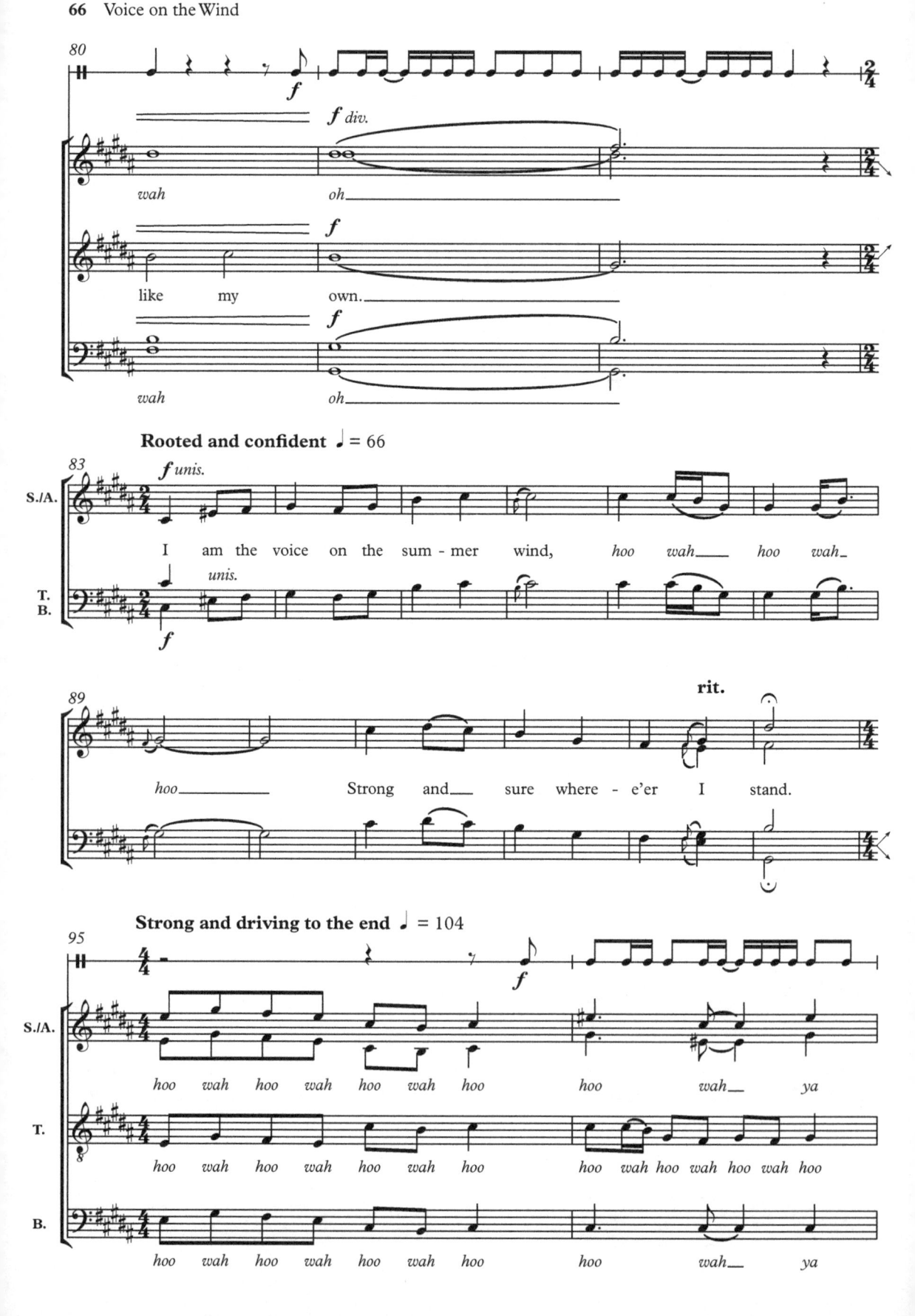
80
f
f div.
wah
oh
f
like my own.
f
wah
oh
Rooted and confident ♩ = 66
83
f unis.
S./A.
I am the voice on the sum - mer wind, hoo wah hoo wah
T.
B.
unis.
f
89
rit.
hoo Strong and sure where - e'er I stand.
Strong and driving to the end ♩ = 104
95
f
S./A.
hoo wah hoo wah hoo wah hoo hoo wah ya
T.
hoo wah hoo wah hoo wah hoo hoo wah hoo wah hoo wah hoo
B.
hoo wah hoo wah hoo wah hoo hoo wah ya

97
hoo wah___ hoo wah___ ya
hoo wah_ hoo wah hoo hoo wah_ hoo wah hoo wah hoo
hoo wah___ ya hoo wah___ ya
99
hoo wah___ I am the
hoo wah hoo wah hoo I am the
hoo wah___ ya I am the
102
ff
voice.
hoo wah hoo wah hoo wah hoo
voice.
hoo wah hoo wah hoo wah hoo
voice.
hoo wah hoo wah hoo wah hoo

Commissioned by the Agincourt Singers (James Pinhorn, Conductor)
in celebration of the one hundredth anniversary of the Agincourt Collegiate Institute

I know a bank where the wild thyme blows

William Shakespeare
from *A Midsummer Night's Dream* (Act 2, Scene 1)

SARAH QUARTEL

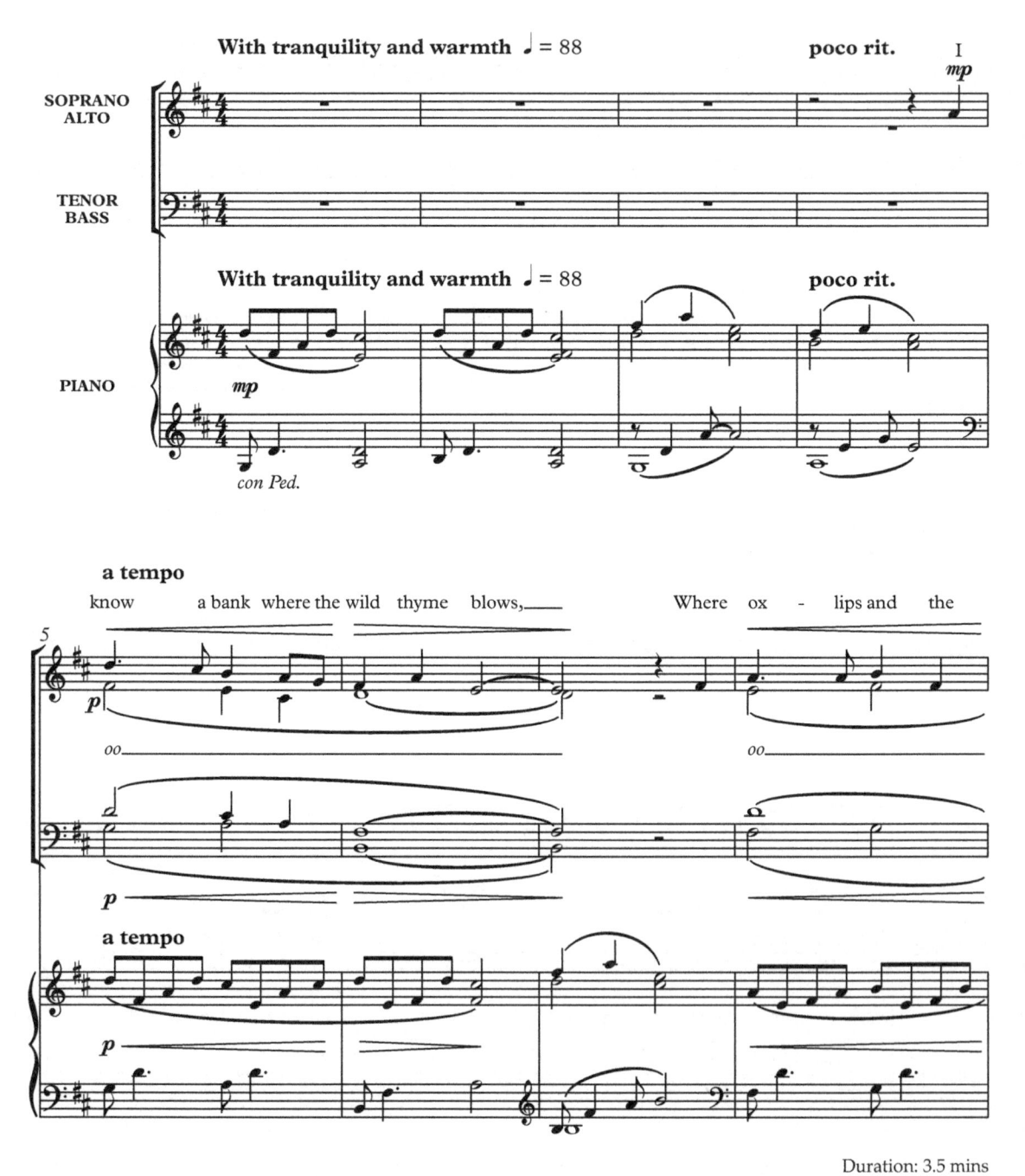

Duration: 3.5 mins

Originally published in *Shall I compare thee?* (ISBN 978–0–19–340614–8).

© Oxford University Press 2015. Photocopying this copyright material is ILLEGAL.

* *eglantine* = sweet briar, a species of wild rose

know a bank where the wild thyme blows.
20
oo
24
mf
There sleeps Ti - tan - ia some-time of the night,
mf
mf legato
28
3
Lulled in these flo - wers with dan - ces and de - light;
f
And
flo - wers

* *throws* = sheds, † *weed* = garments

43
ox - lips and the nod - ding vio - let grows,
mp
46
Quite o - ver - can - o - pied with lus - cious
49
wood - bine, With sweet musk -
mp

52
- ros - es, and with eg - lan - tine.
I
mp
poco rit.
55
mf
mp
know a bank where the wild thyme blows,
the
mf
mp
poco rit.
mf
59
rit.
dim.
p
wild thyme blows.
dim.
p
rit.
mp
dim.
p
Ped.

One of these Days

Words and music by
SARAH QUARTEL

Duration: 4 mins

* The piano reduction includes the rhythmic accompanying parts throughout; for reasons of playability, melodic lines are sometimes omitted.

© Oxford University Press 2021. Photocopying this copyright material is ILLEGAL.

11
days go by, when to-mor - row is all that you live.
doo doo doo doo - n doo doo doo doo - n doo - n doo oh
doo doo doo doo - n doo doo doo doo - n doo - n doo oh
doo doo doo doo - n doo doo doo doo - n doo - n doo oh
doo doo doo
16
Is - n't it a - maz - ing how these years go by, gone
oo doo doo doo doo - n doo doo doo doo - n
oo doo doo doo doo - n doo doo doo doo - n
oo doo doo doo doo - n doo doo doo doo - n
doo doo doo doo doo doo

21
(opt. SOLO or SMALL GROUP)
(TUTTI) mf
S. 1
be - fore they be - gin.
ha oo
(opt. SOLO or SMALL GROUP)
mf
S. 2
be - fore they be - gin.
Is - n't it a-
A.
doo doo doo doo - n doo - n doo oh oo doo doo
mf
T.
doo doo doo doo - n doo - n doo oh oo doo doo
doo doo doo doo - n doo - n doo oh oo doo doo
mf
BAR.
B.
doo doo doo doo doo doo doo doo
mf
26
ha oo
- maz-ing how these dreams go by, when you're wait - ing for them to come.
doo doo - n doo doo doo doo - n doo doo doo doo - n
doo doo - n doo doo doo doo - n doo doo doo doo - n
doo doo - n doo doo doo doo - n doo doo doo doo - n
doo doo doo doo doo doo doo doo doo doo

31
ha oo
Is - n't it a - maz - ing we go on this way,
doo - n doo oh oo doo doo doo doo - n doo doo
doo - n doo oh oo doo doo doo doo - n doo doo
doo - n doo oh oo doo doo doo doo - n doo doo
doo doo doo doo doo doo doo doo doo doo
36
ha oo ah oo
see - ing sha - dows of what could be done.
doo doo - n doo doo doo doo - n doo - n doo oh oo
doo doo - n doo doo doo doo - n doo - n doo oh oo
doo doo - n doo doo doo doo - n doo - n doo oh oo
doo doo doo doo doo doo doo doo

* pronounced 'dye-ya'
† pronounced 'high-ya'

* pronounced 'high-ya'

62
S. 1
S. 2
Breath-ing in the mo-ment is-n't
A.
doo doo-n doo-n doo oh ah oh ah da oh
T.
doo doo-n doo-n doo oh ah oh ah da oh
BAR.
doo doo-n doo-n doo oh ah oh ah da oh
B.
doo doo dn dn dn dn dn doo dn dn dn
67
good e-nough if you be-lieve that hard must be right.
ah da oh ah da oh ah
ah da oh ah da oh ah
ah da oh ah da oh ah
dn dn doo dn dn dn dn dn doo dn dn dn dn dn doo

72
May - be if it's ea - sy it's still worth it all, there's a
da oh May - be if it's ea - sy it's still worth it all, there's a
da oh ah da oh ah da oh
da oh ah da oh ah da oh
dn dn dn dn dn doo dn dn dn dn dn doo dn dn dn
77
cresc. poco a poco
S. 1
dia - mond deep in the fire. ah
S. 2
dia - mond deep in the fire. So one of these days I'm gon-na
A.
dia - mond deep in the fire.
T.
ah da oh ah da oh ah da
AR.
ah da oh ah da oh ah da
B.
dn dn doo dn dn dn dn dn doo dn dn dn dn dn doo
3

82
fly a - way, I'm gon - na fly a - way.
So one of these days, so one of these days, oh
da - n da da da da - n da da da da - n
da - n da da da da - n da da da da - n
dn dn dn dn dn doo dn dn dn dn dn doo dn dn dn
87
ah
So one of these days when I find my way I'll
ah ya oh ah
da da - n da oh ah da da - n da da
da da - n da oh ah da da - n da da
dn dn doo dn dn dn dn dn doo dn dn dn dn dn doo

92
ha ya
find it's to - day. yeah yeah yeah yeah And
ya
da da - n da da da - n da da da da da
da da - n da da da - n da da da da da
dn dn dn dn dn doo dn dn dn dn dn dn doo dn doo doo doo
97
f
may - be we'll see that to - day is e - nough and this
May - be we'll see that to - day is e - nough and this
May - be we'll see that to - day is e - nough and this
May - be we'll see that to - day is e - nough and this
dn doo doo dn dn dn dn doo doo dn doo doo

* pronounced 'high-ya'

109
can be. ha
beau - ty I know we can be. ha yeah
beau - ty I know we can be. ah
beau - ty I know we can be. oh ah
beau - ty I know we can be. oh ah
dn doo doo dn dn dn dn dn dn dn dn
113
più f
ha da - n da
da - n da da - n da da ha - - n da
na na na na na na na na na
dn dn boo doo doo dn dn boo doo doo dn dn doo doo dn doo dn dn dn boo doo doo

118
da - n da
da - n da da yeah da - n da
na na na na na na na na
na na na na na na na na
na na na na na na na na
dn dn boo doo doo dn dn dn dn dn doo dn dn dn boo doo doo
122
ha
da - n da da ha ha
na na na na na na
na na na na na na
na na na na na na
dn dn boo doo doo dn dn dn doo dn doo doo dn dn boo doo doo

126
mf
na na
one of these days.
mp
doo doo doo doo - n
doo doo doo doo - n
doo doo doo doo - n
dn dn boo doo doo doo doo
131
rit.
hoo ah oo
doo doo doo doo - n doo doo doo doo - n doo - n doo oh oo
doo doo doo doo - n doo doo doo doo - n doo - n doo oh oo
doo doo doo doo - n doo doo doo doo - n doo - n doo oh oo
doo doo doo

Dedicated to Matt Jones.
Welcome home.

The Parting Glass

Trad. Scottish
arr. **SARAH QUARTEL**

Duration: 3 mins

A composer's note is available on the OUP website.

Also available in a version for TTBB unaccompanied (ISBN 978–0–19–352746–1).

© Oxford University Press 2018 and 2021. Photocopying this copyright material is ILLEGAL.

8
S.
A.
T.
B.
mf
done, a - las it was to none but me. And
mf
12
all I've done for want of wit to mem - 'ry now I
15
mp
So
can't re - call; fill to me the part - ing
mp
19
If
(mp)
glass, good night and joy be with you all.

23
S.
I had mo-ney e-nough to spend, and lei-sure time to
A.
If I had mo-ney e-nough to spend, lei-sure time to
B.
If I had mo-ney e-nough to spend, lei-sure time to
26
sit a-while, There is a fair maid in this town that
sit a-while, There is a fair maid in this town that
sit a-while, There is a fair maid in this town that
29
S.
A.
sore-ly has my heart be-guiled. Her ros-y cheeks and
T.
B.

32
mp
ru - by lips, I own she has my heart in thrall. Then
mp
35
fill to me the part - ing glass, good night and joy be
38
mf
with you all. Oh, all the com - rades that
mp
Oh, all the com - rades that
41
e'er I had, they're sor - ry for my
mf
e'er I, e'er I had, sor - ry for my
44
go - ing a - way. And all the sweet-hearts that
mp
go - ing a - way. And all the sweet-hearts, oh, that

46
e'er I had, they'd wish me one more
mf
e'er I, e'er I had, wish me one more
49
f
rit.
day to stay. But since it falls un - to my lot that
f
day to stay. But since it falls un - to my lot that I should,
poco meno mosso
52
mf
I should rise and you should not, I gent - ly rise and
mf
I should rise and you should not, gent - ly rise,
55
mp
soft - ly call, good night and joy be with you
mp
molto rit.
59
mp
p
all, good night and joy be with you all.
mp
p